My First Book of Trains

ALL ABOUT LOCOMOTIVES AND RAILCARS FOR KIDS

KRISTINA A. HOLZWEISS, MSLIS, MA

ROCKRIDGE PRESS

For my husband, Michael,
and my children, Tyler, Riley, and Lexy

In memory of my sister Laryssa

For general information on our other products and services, please contact our Customer Care Department within the United States at (866) 744-2665, or outside the United States at (510) 253-0500.

Hardcover ISBN: 978-1-68539-641-1 | Paperback ISBN: 978-1-68539-495-0 | eBook ISBN: 978-1-68539-688-6

Manufactured in the United States of America

Interior and Cover Designer: Brieanna H. Felschow
Art Producer: Maya Melenchuk
Editor: Sasha Henriques
Production Editor: Holland Baker
Production Manager: Jose Olivera

Photography © iStock, cover (front) and p. 53 (bottom); Shutterstock, pp. cover (back), iv, 4-5, 11 (right), 12, 20, 22, 23, 31, 39, 47, 51, 55, 57, 59, 60, 61, 63; INTERFOTO / Alamy Stock Photo, p. 3; Niday Picture Library / Alamy Stock Photo, p. 6; Science History Images / Alamy Stock Photo, p. 7; SPK / Alamy Stock Photo, p. 9; coward_lion / Alamy Stock Photo, p. 11 (left); Zoonar GmbH / Alamy Stock Photo, p. 13; tony french / Alamy Stock Photo, p. 15; Richard Tadman / Alamy Stock Photo, p. 17; Rob Carter / Alamy Stock Photo, p. 18; John Bentley / Alamy Stock Photo, p. 19; Kirn Vintage Stock / Alamy Stock Photo, p. 27; catnap / Alamy Stock Photo, p. 29; Roy LANGSTAFF / Alamy Stock Photo, p. 33; Bruce Leighty / Alamy Stock Photo, p. 35; Matthias Scholz / Alamy Stock Photo, p. 36; imageBROKER / Alamy Stock Photo, p. 37; Jui-Chi Chan / Alamy Stock Photo, p. 41; Robert Timoney / Alamy Stock Photo, p. 43; Classic Image / Alamy Stock Photo, p. 45; Brandon Klein / Alamy Stock Photo, p. 48; Helen Sessions / Alamy Stock Photo, p. 53 (top).

10 9 8 7 6 5 4 3 2 1 0

This Book Belongs to:

_____

Train on a bridge

All Aboard!

Long ago, people traveled by horse. Today, people ride on *trains*. Some trains are even as fast as race cars! There are trains that travel from state to state and country to country. Trains can travel over bridges, underground, and even underwater. Would you like to learn more about trains?

Do you see the metal part in front of the train? This is called a cowcatcher. It clears the tracks when the train moves.

Five hundred years ago, horses and people pulled wagons on tracks called wagonways to move heavy things. Now engines pull railcars to move people and goods like food, supplies, and animals.

Wagonway

Track with two rails

In 1869, the Transcontinental Railroad connected the East and West Coasts. Before it was built, traveling between the coasts took six months. This railroad shortened the journey to one week!

How Trains Work

Railroad tracks guide the train. Most tracks have two rails that are connected by railroad ties. Railroad tracks used to be made from wood, but now they are made from steel. Steel is stronger than wood. Steel tracks can be straight or curved. Train wheels roll on the tracks.

Central Pacific Railroad train Jupiter (Number 60) and Union Pacific Railroad train (Number 119) connect on the Transcontinental Railroad.

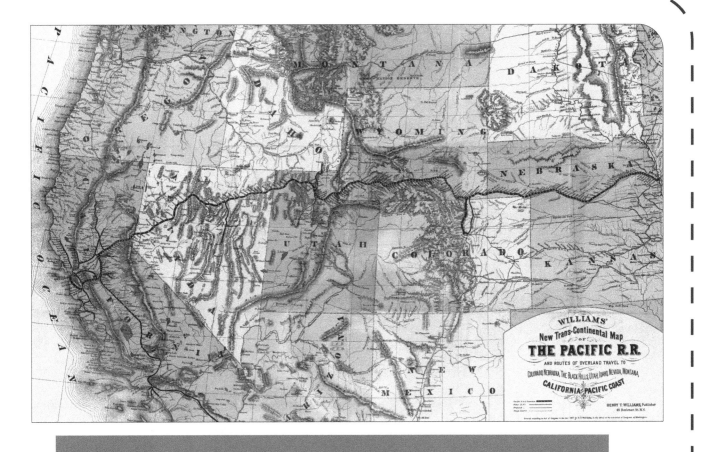

North America's first transcontinental railroad was a
1,776-mile continuous railroad line constructed between
1863 and 1869. It connected the existing eastern U.S. rail
network in Iowa with the Pacific coast in California.

Train wheels are connected with metal rods called **axles**. An axle keeps the wheels moving together. Train engines in the past moved only by **steam**. Today, we have **diesel** and **electric** trains.

Name: Catch Me Who Can
Type: Steam locomotive, passenger
Year Built: 1808
Speed: 12 miles per hour

Who's Who

Do you know who keeps trains moving? A **station** master is in charge of the train station. Conductors check tickets and collect money. Engineers drive the trains. Firemen add wood, oil, or coal to the **firebox**. Signalmen control the signals. Brakemen slow down the trains. Mechanics fix the trains.

Train conductor

Train engineer

Types of Trains

There are many kinds of trains. Each train has a special job. **Passenger** trains help people travel. Have you ever ridden on a passenger train? **Freight** trains carry goods. The power for each train can come from coal, wood, oil, electricity, or magnets.

Passenger train

Name: Big Boy
Type: Freight, steam train
Year Built: 1941
Size: 132 feet 9¼ inches
Speed: 80 miles per hour

Locomotives

A **locomotive** is a special railcar with an engine that makes it move on its own. The first kind was a steam locomotive. It made energy by burning fuel. Other kinds of locomotives are diesel, electric, and magnetic. You will learn more about these different locomotives later.

Name: Mallard
Type: Steam, passenger train
Year Built: 1938
Size: 70 feet long
Speed: 126 miles per hour

A train has at least one locomotive and one other railcar. Locomotives pull the railcars. Sometimes a train has more than one locomotive if there are many railcars or if they are very heavy. A locomotive can push from the back. Heavy trains use locomotives in the middle, too.

One locomotive in Australia pulled almost 700 railcars! The train was 4.6 miles long.

Steam Trains

When you boil water, steam comes out. This is how a steam engine works. Firemen take wood, coal, or oil from the tender. They put it in the firebox, and it burns. The water in the **boiler** heats up and it becomes steam. The steam goes into tubes called **cylinders**.

Some steam engines have **pistons**. Pistons go back and forth. They make the wheels turn and roll on the rails. A **valve** pushes the steam to one end of a piston. Then the valve pushes the steam to the other end. Some steam engines don't have pistons. Instead, they use parts that spin like windmills.

Parts of a steam locomotive

Name: Flying Scotsman
Type: Steam, passenger train
Year Built: 1923
Size: 70 feet long
Speed: 100 miles per hour

Electric streetcar

*The first electric train was invented
by Ernst Werner von Siemens in 1879.
It only traveled 4 miles per hour!*

Electric Trains

Electric trains use electric **motors** to move the wheels. Some trains get electricity from a third rail on the track. Other trains get electricity from wires called **cables**. Newer trains can also get electricity from batteries. Batteries are charged when trains go under electric cables.

Electric train

Electric trains are better for the environment because they don't make smoke. Smoke is bad for the air and for our lungs. Electric trains are also quieter and faster. But electric rails cost more to build. Subways, monorails, cable cars, and trolleys all use electricity.

Monorail

Electro-motive diesel locomotive

Rudolf Diesel invented the diesel engine in 1893.
Before that, he worked on refrigerators!

Diesel Trains

Some engines burn diesel fuel, which has more energy in it than gas. The diesel fuel powers a **generator** that makes electricity for the motors. The motors turn the wheels. Diesel locomotives have more power than steam locomotives and don't need to carry water. They also don't need rails or cables to make electricity.

Freight Trains

Freight trains are strong. They are used to move things very far. They can carry more goods than trucks and planes. These goods can be as small as sand or bigger than elephants. Freight trains can also carry liquids. Some freight trains are very heavy and need more than one locomotive to move. Freight trains don't run on a schedule—they only travel when they are needed.

Circus train

Large circuses used
to travel by freight
train. This is how they
brought animals safely
from town to town.

Freight trains have a special railcar at the end called a **caboose**. The caboose has a kitchen and a place for workers to sleep. The conductor also has an office in the caboose. From the back of the train, conductors can see if there are any problems.

Freight train with a caboose at the end

Railcars

There are many kinds of freight train railcars. Boxcars have sliding doors and solid roofs. Some boxcars are cold so they can carry food. Tankers carry liquids. Hoppers carry very small pieces of materials. Flatcars don't have walls or roofs. They can carry large shipping containers. Centerbeams carry building materials like beams and logs. Autoracks carry cars.

A skybox is a special railcar for airplane parts. Workers put the large parts on flatcars. Then they put covers on them to protect them.

Tanker

Autorack

There are also different kinds of passenger train railcars. People sit in coach railcars. They eat in dining railcars and sleep in sleeping railcars. Observation railcars have the best views on the train, because they have large windows all around the sides and in the roof. The brake van is where the brakeman stops freight and passenger trains.

Observation railcar

Helper Locomotives

Sometimes trains are too large and heavy to go up mountains. Helper locomotives are attached to the front, middle, or back to help other trains climb. They are controlled by radio signals from the main locomotive so the engineer can drive all of them at once.

In the United Kingdom and Australia, a helper locomotive is called a bank engine.

Helper locomotive

Snow Trains

Snow trains clear tracks when there is a lot of snow or ice. One kind has a plow in front, like a truck, and pushes snow to the sides. Another kind has a blower to blow the snow away. The strongest snow train has a round blade that cuts through deep snow.

Snowblower train

The Union Pacific Railroad built the heaviest snow train. It weighs 367,400 pounds. This is heavier than most blue whales!

Mail and Mine Trains

Mail trains had small railcars to move mail quickly underground. They were usually electric. Mine trains were used to move people and tools into and out of mines. They moved by cables. Inside the mines, workers loaded up minecarts with coal or gold. Minecarts were pushed by people or pulled by mules!

Some amusement parks make roller coasters that look like mine trains!

London Mail Rail

Coal mine train

Switcher Locomotives

A **switcher** is a small, slow locomotive that puts railcars together and takes them apart. Then stronger locomotives pull them on the tracks. Sometimes locomotives need to change their direction. They take a ride on a railway **turntable** to spin them around. Broken locomotives can also be repaired in the **roundhouse** around the turntable.

Did you know that you can ride the **Hogwarts Express** *train from the Harry Potter movies in real life? It is called* **The Jacobite** *steam train, and it is located in Scotland.*

Railway turntable with switcher locomotives in a roundhouse

Railroad Cranes

A railroad crane is a crane on a flatbed railcar. Railroad cranes lift freight onto trains. They also take heavy goods off trains. Workers use railroad cranes to build or fix tracks. Sometimes railroad cranes are needed to lift trains that have been in accidents.

Big Carl is the largest railroad crane in the world. It is 820 feet tall.

Big Carl crane

Passenger Trains

Passenger trains help people travel to work, visit friends and families, and see new places. They run on a schedule, and they stop at stations where people can get on and get off. Passenger trains are usually faster than freight trains.

Grand Central Station, New York City

Some passenger trains travel short distances, and others travel from state to state or from country to country. Did you know there are many kinds of passenger trains? There are **commuter** trains, subways, monorails, cable cars and trolleys, long-distance trains, and bullet trains. Let's learn more about these trains.

You can travel from New York to California by train. It will take you about three days to go 3,000 miles!

Passenger train

Commuter train

Commuter Trains

A commuter is a person who travels to work. Commuters on trains can sleep, read, or relax during their journeys. Commuter trains stop at different stations for people to get on and other people to get off. Sometimes commuters switch, or get on other trains.

The Long Island Rail Road is the largest and oldest commuter railroad in the United States operating under its original name.

Subways

Subways help people get around in big cities. They are powered by electricity and run underground. Subway cars only have some seats. Most people stand on subways, and they hold on to poles or straps that hang from the ceiling. Local subways stop at every station. Express subways stop only at some stations so they can travel faster.

The first subway was built in London, England, in 1863. New York City has the most subway stations of any city in the world: 472.

Crowded subway car

Monorails

Monorails run on one rail instead of two. (Mono means one.) The rail can be under or above the cars. Monorails get electricity from the rail. You can see monorails at airports, zoos, and amusement parks. Disneyland in California had the first monorail to run every day in the United States.

About 50 million people ride the Walt Disney World monorail in Florida every year. There are almost 15 miles of rails!

Monorail at Walt Disney World, Florida

A hanging monorail

Cable Cars and Trolleys

Cable cars and trolleys share city streets with cars and people. Cable cars run on steel rails with an open slot between them. They don't have overhead wires. Trolleys also run on steel rails. They get their power from trolley poles connected to a wire above them.

Cable cars were invented in 1873 by Andrew Hallidie to climb the hills of San Francisco. These San Francisco cable cars are the only ones left in the world.

Cable car

Trolley

Long-Distance Trains

People ride on long-distance trains when they travel far distances. Long-distance trains have dining cars where you can eat and sleeping cars with small beds and private bathrooms. The Trans-Siberian Railway is the longest railway in the world. It takes seven days to travel almost 6,000 miles from one end of Russia to the other.

Locomotive P36 is used by the Golden Eagle Luxury Trains private train on the Trans-Siberian Railway.

Name: Locomotive P36
Type: Steam, passenger train
Year Built: 1954
Size: 98 feet, 2 inches long
Speed: 77.7 miles per hour

TRANS-SIBERIAN EXPRESS
100 Years — 100 Лет
ТРАНС-СИБИРСКИЙ ЭКСПРЕСС

Bullet Trains

High-speed passenger trains are called bullet trains. Bullet trains have pointed fronts like airplanes that help them move fast against the wind. Maglev trains are special bullet trains that don't use wheels. They float over guideways using the force of magnets.

Name: Shanghai Maglev bullet train
Type: Magnetic, passenger train
Year Built: 2001
Size: 502 feet long
Speed: 268 miles per hour

Train Safety

Tracks are for trains only. Look both ways at **railroad crossings**. Pay attention to signs, whistles, and signals. Before you cross, wait for the gates to go up and for the lights to stop flashing. When you wait to board a train, don't play on the **platform**. Watch out for the gap when you board a train.

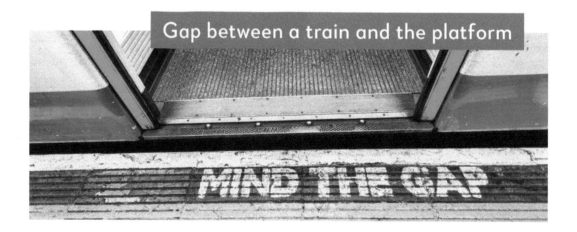

Gap between a train and the platform

MIND THE GAP

Trains and You

If we traveled more by train, there would be fewer accidents, less traffic, and cleaner air. In the future, we might have Hyperloop travel. Groups of people might ride through tubes in small **pods** powered by magnets. These pods would move at almost 800 miles per hour. That is faster than most planes! Aren't trains amazing?

Hyperloop

GLOSSARY

AXLE: A bar that goes through the center of a wheel or group of wheels

BOILER: Where the water in a steam locomotive is held

CABLE: A thick rope made of wire

CABOOSE: The last railcar in a freight train, where the conductor eats, sleeps, and works

COMMUTER: A person who travels to and from work

CYLINDER: The working part of the engine where the piston moves

DIESEL: A fuel that is heavier than gasoline

ELECTRIC: Powered by energy that can build up in one place or flow from one place to another

FIREBOX: Where the fuel is burned in a steam engine

FREIGHT: Cargo carried by a ship, train, truck, or airplane

GENERATOR: A machine that produces electricity or other energy

LOCOMOTIVE: Powered by its own engine; pulls railcars on tracks

MAGLEV: A train powered by magnets

MONORAIL: An electric train that moves on one rail

MOTOR: An electric machine that causes motion or power

PASSENGER: A person who travels

PISTON: Part of an engine that slides in a cylinder to make a machine work

PLATFORM: Where you stand and wait for a train

PODS: High-speed, rounded, railcars that travel in a Hyperloop tube

RADIO SIGNALS: A way of sending sounds or other information through the air

RAIL: The sides of the track on which the train rolls

RAILCAR: The part of a train that is pulled by the locomotive

RAILROAD CROSSING: Where a road crosses railroad tracks

ROUNDHOUSE: A round building where trains are kept and repaired

STATION: A place where trains stop and passengers get on or off, or where freight is loaded or unloaded

STEAM: Hot mist in the air when liquid boils

STEEL: A hard metal used to build with

SUBWAY: Underground electric train

SWITCHER: A locomotive that connects railcars to trains or takes them apart

TRACKS: What trains ride on to guide them

TRAIN: A locomotive pulling one or more railcars

TROLLEY: Trains that run on steel rails and get their power from trolley poles, connected to a wire above them

TURNTABLE: A round platform that spins and helps locomotives change direction

VALVE: Controls the flow of liquid or gas through a tube or pipe

ACKNOWLEDGMENTS

Thank you to my family and friends for always supporting me to pursue my dreams. You have always made me feel like "the little engine that could," even when I felt like I couldn't.

ABOUT THE AUTHOR

 **Kristina A. Holzweiss, MSLIS, MA,** is the 2015 *School Library Journal* School Librarian of the Year, a National School Board "20 to Watch" emerging education technology leader in 2016–2017, and a 2018 *Library Journal* Mover & Shaker. She is a librarian, educator, author, international presenter, library advocate, and keynote speaker. Kristina is the founder of SLIME (Students of Long Island Maker Expo) and a founding member of the Nation of Makers.

Kristina enjoys speaking to librarians, educators and students. Follow Kristina on Twitter at @lieberrian, check out her website bunheadwithducttape.com, or email her at lieberrian@yahoo.com.